BATTLESHIP ISLAND

THE DESERTED ISLAND

BY LISA OWINGS

BELLWETHER MEDIA, MINNEAPOLIS, MN

Are you ready to take it to the extreme?
Torque books thrust you into the action-packed world
of sports, vehicles, mystery, and adventure. These
books may include dirt, smoke, fire, and chilling tales.
WARNING: read at your own risk.

This edition first published in 2018 by Bellwether Media, Inc.

No part of this publication may be reproduced in whole or in part without written
permission of the publisher. For information regarding permission, write to Bellwether
Media, Inc., Attention: Permissions Department, 5357 Penn Avenue South,
Minneapolis, MN 55419.

Library of Congress Cataloging-in-Publication Data

Names: Owings, Lisa, author.
Title: Battleship Island : The Deserted Island / by Lisa Owings.
Description: Minneapolis, MN : Bellwether Media, Inc., [2018] | Series:
   Torque: Abandoned Places | Includes bibliographical references and index.
   | Audience: Ages 7-12. | Audience: Grades 3-7.
Identifiers: LCCN 2016052840 (print) | LCCN 2016052882 (ebook) | ISBN
   9781626176935 (hardcover : alk. paper) | ISBN 9781681034232 (ebook)
Subjects: LCSH: Hashima Island (Japan)–Juvenile literature. | Coal mines and
   mining–Japan–Hashima Island–Juvenile literature. | Ghost
   towns–Japan–Hashima Island–Juvenile literature.
Classification: LCC DS894.99.N339 H3736 2018 (print) | LCC DS894.99.N339
   (ebook) | DDC 952/.244–dc23
LC record available at https://lccn.loc.gov/2016052840

Editor: Betsy Rathburn   Designer: Brittany McIntosh

Printed in the United States of America, North Mankato, MN.

TABLE OF CONTENTS

VISITING THE GHOSTS OF HASHIMA

Rough waves toss the **ferry** toward
Hashima Island. Your stomach twists as
the island comes into view. It looks like
a battleship forgotten at sea.

You take a wobbly step onto the **pier** as you arrive. Crumbling concrete and heaps of **debris** surround you. Above, hundreds of empty windows offer a dark greeting.

Stormy Seas

Fierce storms often sweep across Hashima. The island's concrete buildings shelter against rain and winds. Tall border walls keep out crushing waves.

The wind howls. Waves crash against the island's walls. You gaze up at the **decaying** apartment buildings. What memories are hidden behind this checkerboard of broken glass?

Paint peels from the walls. Televisions and refrigerators lie rusted and ruined. Plants crowd in wherever they can. You wonder how long it will take for nature to claim this place.

A FORGOTTEN ISLAND

Hashima is a tiny island off the southwestern coast of Japan. Its **sea walls** make it look like a ship sailing the East China Sea. This earned it the nickname Battleship Island.

Hashima Island, Japan

Let the Sky Fall

In the 2012 James Bond movie *Skyfall*, Battleship Island is the villain's hideout. But filming on the island was too dangerous. Instead, the crew created sets to capture its chilling feel.

Nagasaki is the nearest Japanese city. From there, the island is less than an hour away by ferry. Yet Hashima feels like part of another world.

In the late 1800s, the promise of coal brought people to Hashima. Thousands of **miners** moved there with their families. By the 1950s, Hashima was the most crowded place on Earth.

Today, the island stands deserted. **Tourists** are its only visitors. How was a place once so full of life so quickly forgotten?

Visiting Hashima

Tourists have been allowed on Hashima since 2009. They must keep to a short walkway. The rest of the island is unsafe.

INTO THE MINES

In the 1800s, the world was hungry for coal. This fuel powered ships, trains, and all kinds of new machines. Hashima sat atop thousands of tons of it.

Hashima's first **mine** opened in 1887. The Mitsubishi company bought it and sent workers there from the **mainland**. The miners risked their lives to dig coal from the **seabed**.

Explore Online

In 2013, Google brought Hashima to the Internet. An employee captured images of the island with a high-tech camera. Now anyone can pay Hashima a virtual visit!

The island's mining business grew quickly. In time, Mitsubishi built concrete apartments so miners could live on the island. Schools, shops, and a hospital also sprouted up.

Still, Hashima was a harsh place. People crowded into small apartments. Workers sweated and suffered in the hot, damp mines. Some worked themselves to death. Others jumped from the island's walls.

The Ghost Island

Hashima is often called a ghost island. Hundreds of workers were sent there never to return.

BATTLESHIP ISLAND TIMELINE

1887:
First coal mine
opens on Hashima

1916:
Japan's first concrete
apartment building is
built on Hashima

1890:
Mitsubishi buys Hashima mine

During **World War II**, Hashima's mines were in full swing. They produced more than 400,000 tons of coal a year. By 1959, the tiny island was home to 5,259 people. Miners worked, played, and raised their children there.

Yet it didn't last. Fifteen years later, only broken pieces of their lives remained. Why was the island abandoned?

1939:
Start of World War II increases demand for coal

1974:
Mitsubishi closes the coal mine on Hashima

1959:
Hashima reaches peak population of 5,259 people

LEFT BEHIND

By the 1970s, coal was no longer Japan's main fuel source. Hashima's coal was almost gone. In January 1974, Mitsubishi closed the mines.

The mining families left quickly. They wanted
to beat the rush for new jobs on the mainland.
By April, the last living soul had left the island.

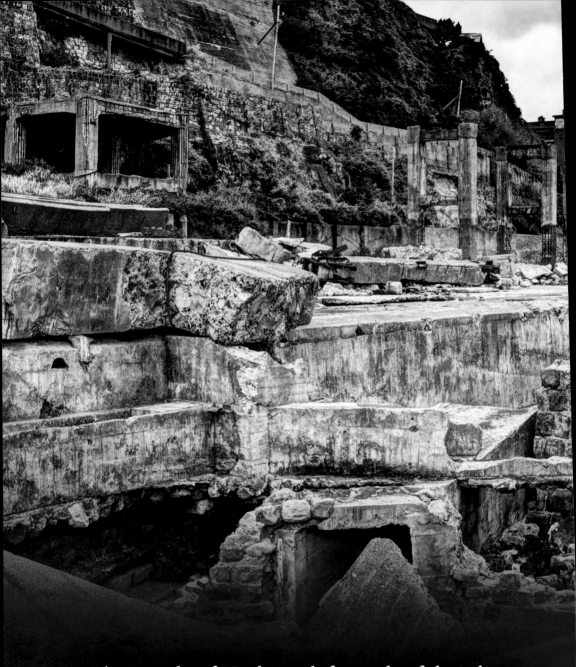

The people of Hashima left much of their lives behind. Dishes still wait to be cleared from tables. Toys and books gather dust. Drawers and cabinets have stood open since moving day.

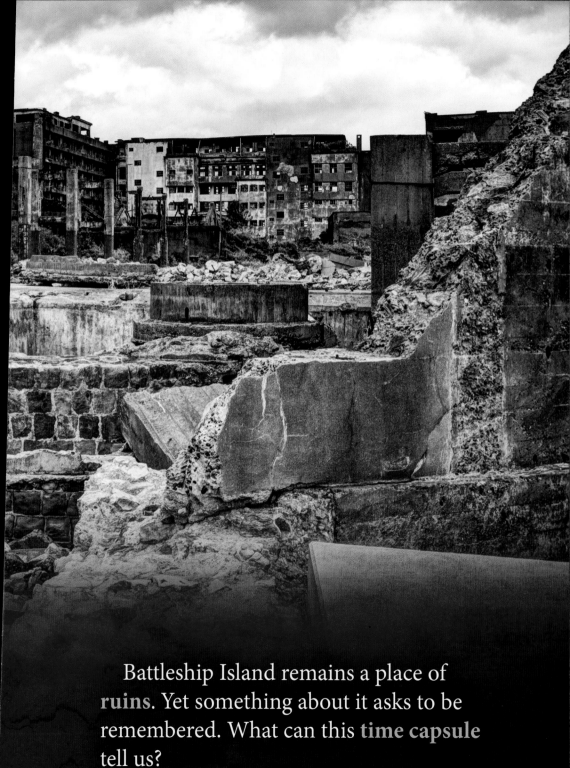

Battleship Island remains a place of
ruins. Yet something about it asks to be
remembered. What can this **time capsule**
tell us?

GLOSSARY

debris—pieces of something destroyed

decaying—slowly breaking down through natural processes

ferry—a boat that carries people and goods from one place to another

mainland—the main part of a continent or land mass

mine—an underground tunnel or pit from which coal or another mineral is taken

miners—workers who dig for coal and other natural resources

pier—a structure that reaches into water and serves as a landing place

ruins—the remains of human-made structures

sea walls—walls built to keep sea waves from spilling onto or destroying the land

seabed—the ocean floor

time capsule—something that stores items from the past or present until they are rediscovered in the future

tourists—people who travel to visit another place

World War II—a war fought from 1939 to 1945

TO LEARN MORE

AT THE LIBRARY

Mullenbach, Cheryl. *The Industrial Revolution for Kids: The People and Technologies that Changed the World.* Chicago, Ill.: Chicago Review Press, 2014.

Nelson, S.D. *Digging a Hole to Heaven: A Story about the Coal Mine Boys.* New York, N.Y.: Abrams Books for Young Readers, 2014.

Williams, Dinah. *Creepy Islands.* New York, N.Y.: Bearport Publishing Company, 2015.

ON THE WEB

Learning more about Battleship Island is as easy as 1, 2, 3.

1. Go to www.factsurfer.com.

2. Enter "Battleship Island" into the search box.

3. Click the "Surf" button and you will see a list of related web sites.

With factsurfer.com, finding more information is just a click away.

INDEX

The images in this book are reproduced through the courtesy of: The Asahi Shimbun, front cover, pp. 7, 10, 12-13, 14, 15; Hemis/ Alamy, pp. 4, 11; Piti Tantaweevongs/ Alamy, p. 5; Michael Runkel/ robertharding/ SuperStock, p. 6; JTB MEDIA CREATION, Inc./ Alamy, pp. 8-9; snotch/ Flickr, pp. 16-17; leungchopan, pp. 18-19; Sean Pavone, pp. 20-21.